Acknowledgments

For their unfailing support and the joy they bring to my life, I dedicate this

collection to my favourite Bermuda treasures, to my wife Diane, daughters

Heidi and Lisa, and grandchildren, Ashley, Kaelan, Justin and Keanu.

I would also like to thank my associates, Joe & Harold Pimental for their continuing support.

Published and distributed in Bermuda by:
Roland Skinner, Picturesque
The Design Centre, 129 Front Street East
Hamilton, HM12, Bermuda

ISBN 976-8160-74-8

Second Edition

10 9 8 7 6 5 4 3 2

Project Managed and Coordinated by:
Laura H. Couallier
Laura Herrmann Design
245 South Maitland Avenue, Suite 212
Maitland, Florida 32751

Written and Edited by:
Don McGregor
Ottawa, Canada

Design and Production:
Laura H. Couallier

Printed in Hong Kong:
Paramount

Picturesque BERMUDA

VOLUME II

Table of CONTENTS

LASTING

IMPRESSIONS

MORE THAN

A PASSING

GLANCE

INTRODUCTION

6

8

54

THE

ARTIST'S

EYE

THE

GLOAMING

INDEX

96

126

160

INTRODUCTION

A Place in the Heart

AN ENCOUNTER WITH BERMUDA'S BEAUTY MAKES AN IMPRESSION that lasts a lifetime. I wonder if this is why so many visitors return again and again, seeking to recapture the feast of the senses offered by one of the planet's most harmonious blends of natural and human creation.

Arriving by air as most people do, whether from North America or Europe, is to sense that you are entering a special place. As a child, I formed a vague notion of Bermuda from occasional mentions in newspapers, memories of family friends who had honeymooned there, and images of the billowing sails of sleek racing yachts. Many years later, when I caught my first sight of the Island, I was struck that such a place, protected only by sturdy coral reefs in the midst of the vast blue of the Atlantic, had touched the lives of so many people in so many faraway places. My expectations were also fueled by myths and images from the many notable writers and artists whose imaginations have been seized by Bermuda's charms, not to overlook the everyday reactions of friends and acquaintances whose spirits always seem to be buoyed at the very mention of the place. But no amount of anticipation could prepare me for what I found.

Most memorable is the first rush of the senses coming alive to surroundings for which no ordinary vocabulary is sufficient. The American writer Mark Twain, who spent much of his later life on the Island, said that Bermuda is as close to heaven as most of us will ever know. On first encounter, many lesser mortals find themselves incapable of finding words to express an overwhelming sensory awakening. And many a visual artist from "away" has found that a palette of colour adequate to other climes is incapable of rendering the sub-tropical light that paints Bermuda.

Bermuda's twenty-one square miles features an array of sturdy pastel-coloured buildings with whitewashed slate roofs that make a bold statement of the Island's character. Long ago Bermudians learned to appreciate and respect the forces of nature that bring the soothing breezes and warm currents of the Gulf Stream but, from time to time, threaten with the fury of wind and wave. The result is an architecture that blends practical and aesthetic needs in a unique style that makes one of Bermuda's most memorable impressions.

What Bermudians have created and the emerald green of the Island's lush vegetation are set against a background of rock and sea. Houses with welcoming moongates perch ingeniously on rocky outcroppings overlooking the ever-changing ocean. The celebrated Bermuda cottage and magnificent family homes, shaded by elegant Bermuda cedars, sit amidst greenery protected by palmettos and punctuated by banana and orange trees and the native Bermudiana flower. Turquoise waters lap beaches pink-tinged by coral, oases that catch the eye like sparkling gems on a necklace strung around the Island, and harbours large and small shelter seagoing craft of all sizes and styles. Narrow stone-fenced roadways link it all together, winding like ribbons through a maze of green vegetation, agricultural fields, forest groves and grey rock.

Bermuda is at once rugged and attuned to the sea and as delicate as the fresh blooms of freesia, poinciana, nasturtium, frangipani, lily and bougainvillaea, among a multitude of species. They catch the eye with a kaleidoscope of whites, blues, oranges, deep reds, yellows and mauves, and scent the air with their delicate perfumes. Here a cascading bank of pink oleander lends privacy to a home, and there a single red geranium set against the background of a deep green Bermuda shutter transforms an ingenious invention into a work of art.

Bermudians live their art by expressing a joyous sensitivity to their surroundings in every aspect of Island life. They adopt colourful styles of dress for business and social encounters, and cultivate gardens that enhance life at home and please the eye of passers-by. Bermudians use colour to highlight everything they make and do, sometimes muted to better reflect the changing light of sun, sea and sky, and other times jubilantly responding to the beauty of the natural world, as they do with the thousands of hand-crafted multi-coloured kites that soar over the Island every Good Friday.

To be in Bermuda is to live at a level of heightened awareness that grows in response to the long slow rustling of waves rising and receding over a sandy beach, the stirring thunder of wave against rock, the questioning chirp of the Kiskadee— "Qu'est-ce qu'il dit?"—and the awe-inspiring flight of the Bermuda longtail, soaring high and swooping low to skim the surface of the sea.

The deepening shades of late afternoon and a stillness in the air herald the sunset. When darkness descends over the Island the heat of day abates as evening breezes sigh through the cedars, and you feel that you could reach up for a handful of stars. The echo of the tree-frogs singing in the cool night air completes a daily cycle that harmonizes the rhythms of inner and outer life.

What Bermudians have created on top of a submarine mountain—an ancient, extinct volcano of the undersea range that bisects the Atlantic deep—takes on subtle variations under the always changing influences of nature. If you were to pick one place to fix your gaze every second of every minute of every day of a Bermuda year, you would never see the same image twice, never sense the same fragrances, the same sounds, the same feeling of wind on your face. And next year it would start all over again, and none of the permutations of sight, sound, fragrance and texture would ever repeat.

The sense of being at one with your surroundings must be why the Bermuda experience calls to so many people in so many faraway places as they hurry through life, marching to the insistent beat of a far different drum. Amidst the pressures and distractions of routine days, a desire for return and renewal stirs intimations of a place like no other.

Roland Skinner is an artist fully alive to Bermuda's splendour, always seeking to capture its infinite variety in images suffused with the love he feels for his Island home. I turn to his work in a world far from Bermuda's shores to evoke the joys and satisfactions of a place that lives in my heart every moment of every day.

Don McGregor, Ottawa, Canada

Don McGregor is a Canadian writer and public servant who lived and worked in Bermuda from 1988 to 1990.

More than a Passing Glance

HE MORE YOU SEE IN BERMUDA, THE MORE THERE IS TO SEE, FOR THE ISLAND seems to have been touched in all its aspects by a designer's hand. Those who look deeper find that beauty fills the eye of the beholder.

Splashes of coloured blossoms spill over rock fences that line the roadways. Rough, pitted rock shelters a beach and, just below, an asymmetrical line made by an ascending gentle wave darkens the sand for an instant, and then, as the wave recedes, the sparkling pink tinge returns.

The turquoise of the shallow waters over coral gives way to the cobalt blue of miles-deep ocean and, at the horizon, cloud-piled skies meet froth-tipped waves. A watery archway appears for a moment as the impenetrable shoreline throws back a surge of surf.

A gently curving path softens the approach to the sturdy geometry of a Bermudian home. Horizontal lines of steps curve upwards against a vertical beige wall lit by the sun and patterned by the shade of clouds. And a bank of blooms red, yellow and pink, reaches towards the wide stripes of a whitewashed slate roof.

Patterns, patterns everywhere. Pause and look to savour Bermuda's deeper rewards.

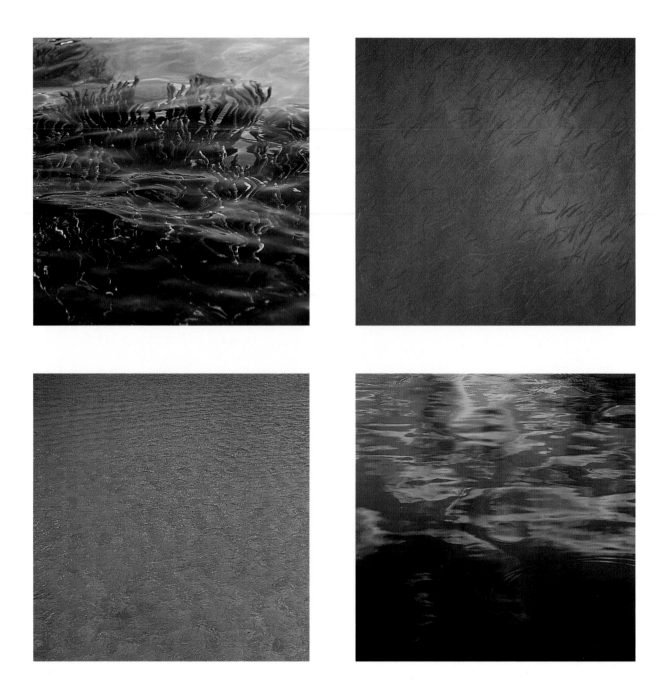

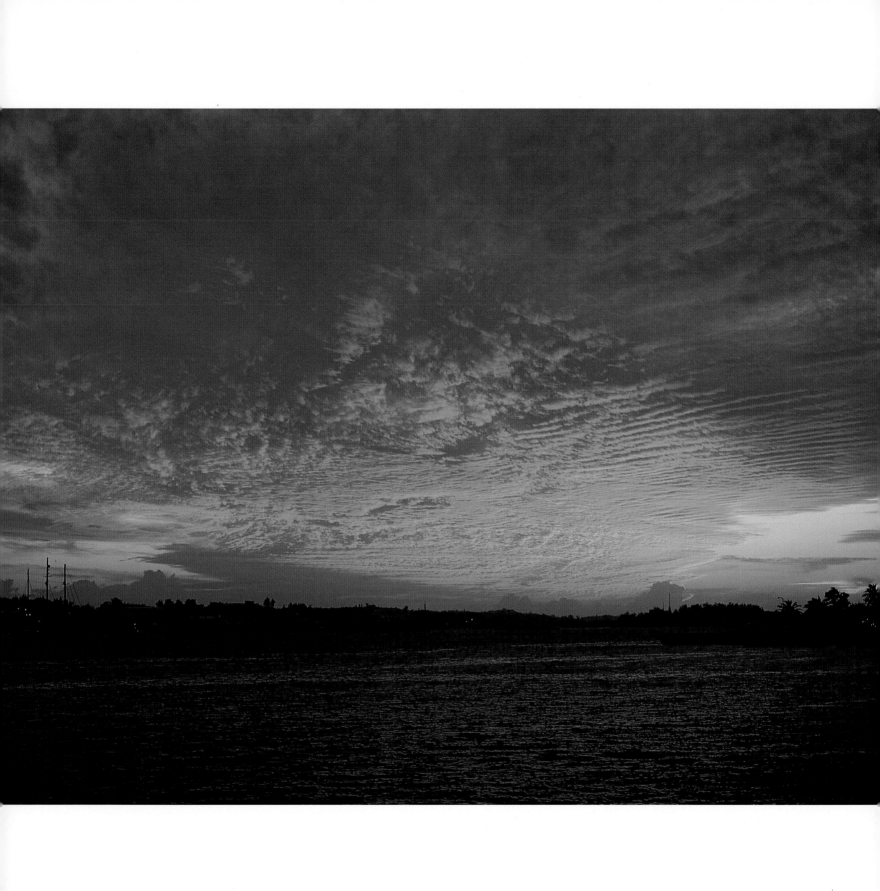

The Gloaming

LATE AFTERNOON, THE SEAS ARE CALM AND THE WINDS DIE DOWN, THE SUN SINKS TOWARDS THE horizon, and colours that faded in the glare of blazing midday become muted, tinged and deeply enriched as shadows fall and the pace of life slows. These are the golden hours Bermudians treasure as "the gloaming."

Latestayers are reluctant to leave the beach. They linger to savour the warm waters and delights of day's end. From St. George's in the east to Dockyard in the west, in every parish, a hush falls, voices lower and quiet times descend as outward calm brings inner peace.

It is Bermuda's most satisfying time, rich with changing colour as the angled rays of the sun sparkle the calm surface of the sea with diamonds of light, the chirping of the birds fades, soon to be replaced for the night by the soothing rhythmic chorus of the tree frogs.

At ground level, the light fades to darkness, but the tops of trees, lighthouses and buildings provide a bright contrast as they catch the sun's last rays. Suddenly, the sun slides below the red-pink glow of the horizon. The gloaming provides the perfect end of day, for Bermudians know that the sun also rises, and tomorrow will bring new beauty to delight the senses and enrich the spirit.

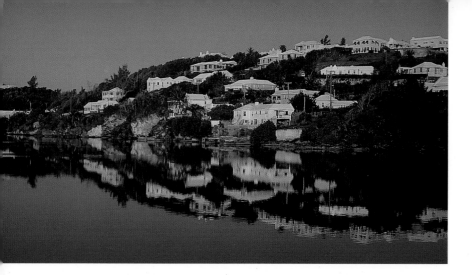

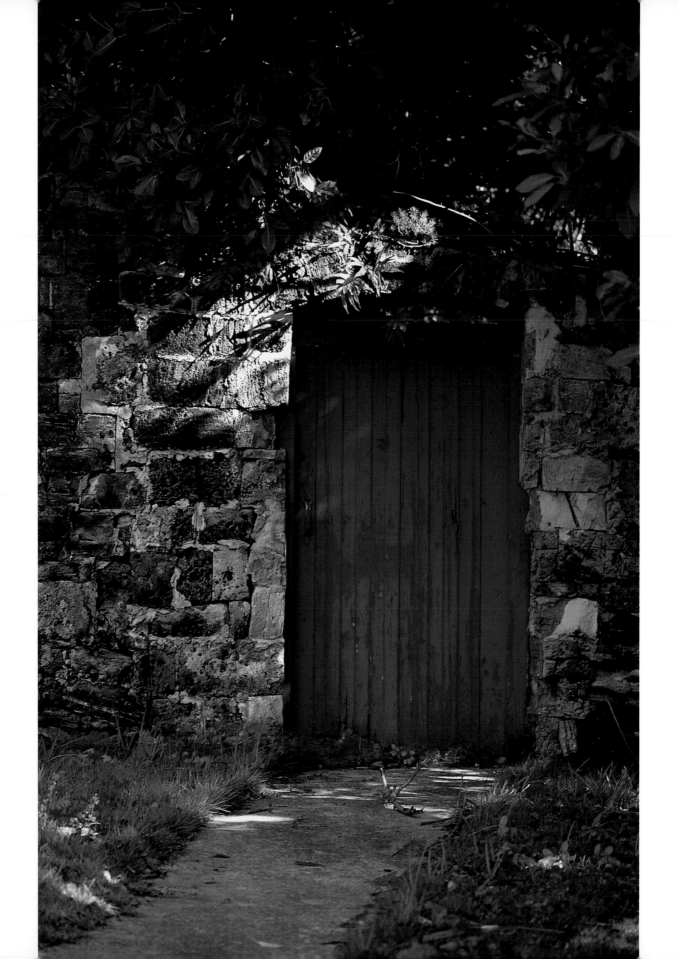

INDEX

P. 1	Sea and Sand Patterns	P. 52-53	Pembroke Rectory, Pembroke	P. 110	Roof Line, St. George's
P. 2	Watch Hill Park, Smiths	P. 54	Newstead, Paget	P. 111	Fence, St. George's
P. 4-5	Carter House Roof, St. David's	P. 56-57	Grape Bay, Paget	P. 112-113	left to right: Oleander, Hibiscus, Lily, Water Lily
P. 6	Island From Southwest	P. 58	Ely's Harbour, Somerset	P. 114-115	Old Church, Hamilton Parish
P. 8	Pomander Road, Paget	P. 59	Coney Island, St. George's	P. 116-117	Palms
P. 10-11	Kings Point, Somerset	P. 60	Pompano Beach Club, Southampton	P. 118	Watergate, Southampton
P. 12	Beach Near Horseshoe Bay, Southampton	P. 61	Ariel Sands Club, Devonshire	P. 119	Bermuda Window
P. 13	left: Beach Near Horseshoe Bay, Southampton; right: The Reefs Beach, Southampton	P. 62	Fanny Fox's Cottage, St. George's	P. 120-121	North Shore Sunset, Devonshire
		P. 63	Queen St, St. George's	P. 122	clockwise from top left: Coreopsis, Lantana, Morning Glory, Sprekelia
P. 14	Nonsuch Island, St. George's	P. 64	Landscape, Southampton		
P. 15	Kings Point, Somerset	P. 65	Landscape, Southampton	P. 123	clockwise from top left: Dahlia, Iris, Amaryllis, Nasturtium
P. 16	Pitts Bay, Pembroke	P. 66-67	Water Reflections		
P. 17	Norwood Boat House, Pembroke	P. 68	Pampus Grass	P. 124	The Reefs, Southampton
P. 18	Nonsuch Island, St. George's	P. 69	Spider Lilies, Southampton	P. 125	left: Spanish Point, Pembroke, right: Flatts, Smiths
P. 19	left: Frick's Point, St. George's; right: Nonsuch Island, St. George's	P. 70-71	Springfield, Somerset		
		P. 72	Gate, Somerset	P. 126	Crowlane Bakery, Pembroke
P. 20	Devonshire Dock, Devonshire	P. 73	Wall, Warwick	P. 128	Cottage, Pembroke
P. 21	Net Fishing, Pigeon Hole, Devonshire	P. 74-75	Cresting Waves, John Smith's Bay	P. 129	left: Harrington Sound, right: Holy Trinity Church
P. 22-23	Laura's View, Devonshire	P. 76	Gibbs Hill Lighthouse, Southampton	P. 130-131	Field of Freesia
P. 24	Western Long Bay, Warwick			P. 132-133	Dockyard, Somerset
P. 25	left: Eastern Horseshoe Bay, Southampton; right: Cathedral Rocks, Somerset	P. 77	St. David's Lighthouse, St. George's	P. 134	Dingles Island, Hamilton Parish
		P. 78-79	Walls and Gates	P. 135	Monroe Beach, Southampton
P. 26	Castle Island, St. George's	P. 80-81	Castle Harbour Beach	P. 136	House, Pomander Rd, Paget
P. 27	Frick's Point, St. George's	P. 82	Riddells Bay Golf Course, 10th. Tee, Southampton	P. 137	Boat House, Pomander Rd, Paget
P. 28-29	Longtail Birds			P. 138	left to right: Path, Smiths; Camden, Devonshire; Arboretum, Devonshire
P. 30-31	The Reefs Beach, Southampton	P. 83	Periwinkle Flowers, St George's		
P. 32	Harrington Sound, Hamilton Parish	P. 84	Riddells Bay Golf Course, 15th. Tee, Southampton	P. 139	left to right: Arboretum, Devonshire; Arboretum, Devonshire; Springfield, Somerset
P. 33	Harrington Sound, Smiths	P. 85	Riddells Bay Golf Course, 15th Tee, Reflection, Southampton		
P. 34	Coney Island, St. George's			P. 140-141	Buttery, Cambridge Beaches, Somerset
P. 35	left: Coney Island; right: Flatts Inlet, Smiths	P. 86-87	Beach Surf, Long Bay, Warwick		
		P. 88	House, Mid Ocean Golf Course	P. 142-143	John Smith Bay, Smiths
P. 36	Fairy Lands, Pembroke	P. 89	Shutter, St. George's	P. 144	Fire Fly Hall, Devonshire
P. 37	Malibar Gate, Pembroke	P. 90-91	Waves	P. 145	Milner House, Devonshire
P. 38	The Reefs Beach, Southampton	P. 92	Arboretum, Devonshire	P. 146	Lizard
P. 39	left: Mid Ocean Cliff; right: Church Bay, Southampton	P. 93	Palm Grove, Devonshire	P. 147	Blue Bird Box
		P. 94	Green Shutters, Paget	P. 148-49	Devonshire Bay, Devonshire
P. 40-41	Railway Trail	P. 95	Pink Shutter, Paget	P. 150	Dockyard, Somerset
P. 42-43	Architecture, St George's	P. 96	Miles Building, Hamilton	P. 151	Grape Bay, Paget
P. 44	left: Frick's Point, St. George's; right: Charles and Castle Islands, St. George's	P. 98-99	Dinghies, Riddells Bay, Southampton	P. 152-153	Quoins and Scallop Gable End, Smiths
		P. 100-101	Walls, Somerset and Pembroke		
P. 45	Tuckers Town, St. George's	P. 102	Ariel Sands Club, Devonshire	P. 154	Gate, Corkscrew Hill, Devonshire
P. 46	Astwood Cove, Warwick	P. 103	left to right: Poinciana, Croaton, Tulips	P. 155	Fairy Lands, Pembroke
P. 47	South Shore, Warwick			P. 156	Sunrise, Trimingham Hill, Paget
P. 48	Devonshire Marsh, Devonshire	P. 104	Hamilton Harbour, Pembroke	P. 157	Sunrise, Grape Bay, Paget
P. 49	Arboretum, Devonshire	P. 105	Trimingham Hill, Paget	P. 158-159	Sunrise, Natural Arches Beach
P. 50-51	Mermaid Beach, South Shore, Warwick	P. 106-107	Surinam Cherries		
		P. 108-109	Colourful Roof Lines